SCHOLASTIC

Scholastic Success With
Spelling

Grade 2

by Lisa Molengraft

New York • Toronto • London • Auckland • Sydney
Mexico City • New Delhi • Hong Kong • Buenos Aires

Teaching *Resources*

Cover art by Amy Vangsgard
Cover design by Maria Lilja
Interior illustrations by Sherry Neidigh
Interior design by Quack & Company

ISBN 0-439-55373-3

Copyright © 2004 Scholastic, Inc.
All rights reserved. Printed in the U.S.A.

12   40   09

Introduction

Parents and teachers alike will find this book to be a valuable learning tool. The book is organized into 21 lists, each following a phonetic spelling rule. The list words were developed from a collection of age-appropriate, high-priority word lists. At the end of each list you will find three words that can be used as an academic challenge.

Throughout the book you will find the following symbols that represent various strategy-based skills:

 Visual Discrimination Skills: Use this strategy to highlight visual similarities among words.

 Sound Relationship Skills: Use this strategy to highlight sound patterns among words.

 Dictation Skills: Read the dictation sentence aloud to students. Having students write the sentence will provide additional practice in spelling list words as well as practice in using correct punctuation.

 Writing Skills: Use this strategy to practice writing sentences using the list words.

 Reading Skills: These activities include stories and letters with missing words, giving students an opportunity to connect reading with writing.

 Fun Stuff!: This section includes games, puzzles, and codes in which children apply previously learned strategies.

 Challenge Word Activities: This section offers an opportunity to stretch spelling skills to a more difficult level using the three optional challenge words.

 Bright Idea Activities: This section offers extension ideas to bridge beyond "the book" and into "the world."

Throughout the book students will find Review Lists. These are not a collection of "old words," but are actually new list words that follow previously learned patterns. This list gives students a chance to apply mastered skills and strategies.

Through a collection of well-prepared lists, age-appropriate challenges, valuable spelling strategies, and stimulating activities, students will gain the self-confidence they need to become strong spellers.

Table of Contents

Matt's Map

 *The **short**-a **sound** is found in the word **map**.*

Read and copy each list word. Circle the letter that makes the short-*a* sound. Watch for a word with an unexpected silent *e* ending. Then organize the list words by their number of letters.

List Words

1. map
2. ask
3. last
4. has
5. sack
6. clap
7. after
8. mask
9. black
10. have

1. _____
2. _____
3. _____
4. _____
5. _____
6. _____
7. _____
8. _____
9. _____
10. _____

three letters

_____
_____
_____

five letters

_____
_____

four letters

_____
_____
_____
_____
_____

Challenge Words

11. backpack
12. stamp
13. stand

11. _____
12. _____
13. _____

Change one letter in each word to spell a list word. The first one has been done for you.

1. ash ___ask___   2. mash _____   3. slap _____

4. block _____   5. list _____   6. lap _____

7. his _____   8. sick _____   9. hive _____

 <u>Matt</u> <u>has</u> a <u>map</u> in the <u>black</u> <u>sack</u>.

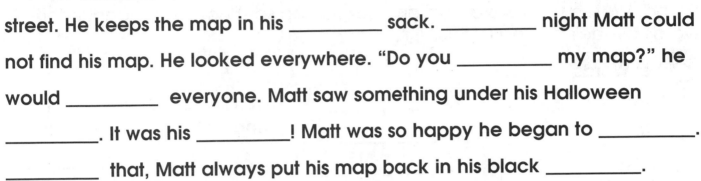

 Use the list words to complete the story.

Matt's Map

Matt _____ a map of the houses on his

street. He keeps the map in his _____ sack. _____ night Matt could

not find his map. He looked everywhere. "Do you _____ my map?" he

would _____ everyone. Matt saw something under his Halloween

_____. It was his _____! Matt was so happy he began to _____.

_____ that, Matt always put his map back in his black _____.

Follow the clues to play tic-tac-toe. As you find each answer, mark an X or O. Do you get three in a row?

1. I am the antonym (opposite) for *answer*. Mark an *X*.
2. I am a color. Mark an *O*.
3. I rhyme with *past*. Mark an *X*.
4. I am the antonym for *before*. Mark an *O*.
5. She ____ a sister. Mark an *X*.
6. I begin like the word *sit*. Mark an *X*.
7. I rhyme with *map*. Mark an *X*.
8. They ____ a dog. Mark an *O*.
9. I rhyme with *ask*. Mark an *X*.

has	have	clap
black	mask	sack
last	after	ask

Write the challenge word that finishes each analogy.

10. You put a plate on the table. You put a _____ on a letter.
11. *Down* is the antonym for *up*. *Sit* is the antonym for _____.
12. A wallet is kept in a purse. A book is kept in a _____.

 Cut letters from an old newspaper and glue them to another sheet of paper to spell each of the list words.

My Backyard Tent

➡️ The **short-**e **sound** *is found in the word* **tent**.

Read and copy each list word. Circle the letter that makes the short-*e* sound. Watch for a word with an unexpected spelling. Then organize the list words by their ending letters.

 List Words

			words that end with *t*	words that end with *d*
1. tent	1. _____		_____	_____
2. met	2. _____		_____	_____
3. send	3. _____		_____	_____
4. went	4. _____		_____	_____
5. bed	5. _____		_____	_____
6. nest	6. _____		_____	
7. bend	7. _____		_____	
8. yet	8. _____			
9. best	9. _____			
10. said	10. _____			

🏆 **Challenge Words**

11. bench	11. _____
12. next	12. _____
13. else	13. _____

 Each list word has a rhyming partner. Write two list words that rhyme.

1. _____   2. _____   3. _____

_____   _____   _____

4. _____   5. _____

_____   _____

 "I <u>went</u> to <u>bed</u> in a <u>tent</u>," said <u>Ned</u>.

Scholastic Teaching Resources

Circle ten misspelled words. Write them correctly on the lines.

My Backyard Tent

My dad and I built a tint in the backyard.

We had to bind sticks to stake it in the

ground. We had the beste time. We made

a bid out of straw. We sed it was like a bird's

nast. My mom said she would sind a snack

out to us. We mete her in the yard and then

she whent back in the house. She said she isn't ready for camping yat!

1. _____   2. _____   3. _____   4. _____

5. _____   6. _____   7. _____   8. _____

9. _____   10. _____

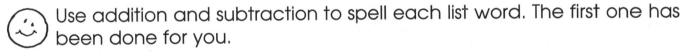 Use addition and subtraction to spell each list word. The first one has been done for you.

11. rest – r + b = ___best___   **12.** test – s + n = _____

13. mat – a + e = _____   **14.** bad – a + e = _____

15. sent – t + d = _____   **16.** sand – n + i = _____

17. send – s + b = _____   **18.** set – s + y = _____

19. next – x + s = _____   **20.** want – a + e = _____

Write the challenge word that matches each definition.

21. another choice _____

22. a place to sit _____

23. the nearest in order _____

 On another sheet of paper, write the list words in order from easiest to hardest to spell.

The Missed Kick

 The **short-i sound** *is found in the word* **miss**.

Read and copy each list word. Circle the letter that makes the short-*i* sound. Then organize the list words by the letter clues.

 List Words

1. hid	**1.** _____	
2. mix	**2.** _____	
3. with	**3.** _____	
4. tip	**4.** _____	
5. milk	**5.** _____	
6. miss	**6.** _____	
7. slip	**7.** _____	
8. kick	**8.** _____	
9. kiss	**9.** _____	
10. pick	**10.** _____	

words that begin with *m*
_____
_____
_____
_____

words that have a *p*
_____
_____
_____
_____

words that begin with *k*
_____
_____

words that have an *h*
_____
_____

 Challenge Words

11. into	**11.** _____
12. trick	**12.** _____
13. sister	**13.** _____

 Circle the word that is spelled correctly.

1. pik	pick	**2.** melk	milk	**3.** kiss	kis
4. tip	tipp	**5.** slep	slip	**6.** kik	kick
7. hid	hidd	**8.** miks	mix	**9.** mis	miss

<u>Did</u> he <u>slip</u> and <u>miss</u> the <u>kick</u>?

Name _____

 Write the list word that matches each clue.

1. I am the past tense of *hide*. I am _____.
2. We rhyme with *sick*. We are _____ and _____.
3. I am part of the dairy food group. I am _____.
4. I begin with the same sound as *wind*. I am _____.
5. I am a synonym for *stir*. I am _____.
6. We rhyme with *flip*. We are _____ and _____.
7. Do this to your mom or dad. I am _____.
8. I am kiss – k + m. I am _____.

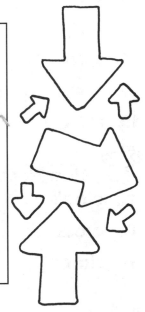

Circle each list word hidden in the puzzle. The words go across, down, or diagonally.

```
g m i l k a j l p w e i c e o
u s o x f x c q b i w f e y z
f l e d m i b t n r c j o d w
p i k i c k p r b m m k i f i
l p i k x a d v c i m i r g t
k u t b d h i d m s r j x n h
v t i p v m g r b s i d i i d
h d i r p n p z k i s s e q i
b c f h a q r t p k a c s h e
```

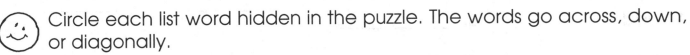

Write the challenge word that finishes each question.

9. Does Josie's _____ share a bedroom with her?
10. Did you stir the milk _____ the cake mix?
11. Have you learned a new magic _____?

 On another sheet of paper, write the list words in alphabetical order.

Socks With Dots

 *The **short-**o **sound** is found in the word **sock**.*

Read and copy each list word. Circle the letter that makes the short *o* sound. Then organize the list words in rhyming pairs.

 List Words

1. sock   1. _____   _____   _____
2. mop   2. _____   _____   _____
3. box   3. _____   _____   _____
4. spot   4. _____   _____   _____
5. odd   5. _____   _____   _____
6. off   6. _____   _____   _____
7. dot   7. _____
8. stop   8. _____   **Which two words do not have a rhyming partner?**
9. fox   9. _____
10. lock   10. _____   _____   _____

 Challenge Words

11. clock   11. _____
12. cross   12. _____
13. stomp   13. _____

 Change the vowel in each word to spell a list word.

1. map _____   2. step _____   3. sack _____

4. fix _____   5. lick _____   6. spit _____

7. add _____

📢 **My <u>sock</u> with <u>dots</u> is in the <u>box</u>.**

Use a list word to complete each analogy.

1. *Pull* is the antonym for *push*. *On* is the antonym for _____.

2. A hat goes on your head. A _____ goes on your foot.

3. Scrub a pan. _____ a floor.

4. A knob opens a door. A key opens a _____.

5. *An* is in *can*. *Ox* is in _____ or _____.

6. *Short* is the antonym for *tall*. _____ is the antonym for *go*.

7. Two, four, and six are even. One, three, and five are _____.

8. A box is square. A _____ is round.

9. A puddle is on the street. A _____ is on the rug.

Complete each puzzle with two list words.

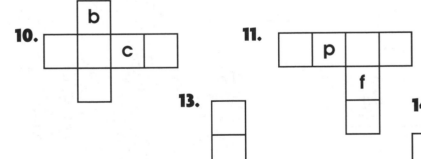

10.

b
c

11.

p
f

12.

k
x

13.

d

14.

t
p

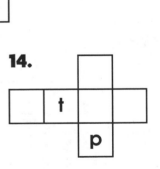

Write each challenge word three times.

_____   _____   _____

_____   _____   _____

_____   _____   _____

 Find the list words written in some of your favorite books.

Scholastic Teaching Resources

A Bump in the Road

 The **short-u sound** *is found in the word* **bump.**

Read and copy each list word. Circle the letter that makes the short-*u* sound. Watch for words that use unexpected spellings. Then organize the list by the letters making the short-*u* sound.

 List Words   *u*   *a*

1. rub   1. _____ _____
2. bump   2. _____ _____
3. come   3. _____ _____   *o*
4. was   4. _____ _____
5. dump   5. _____ _____
6. must   6. _____
7. from   7. _____
8. dust   8. _____   *o_e*
9. tub   9. _____
10. some   10. _____

Challenge Words

11. lunch   11. _____
12. stuck   12. _____
13. stung   13. _____

 Write a list word that begins with the same sound as the picture.

1. _____   2.  _____   3. _____

4. _____   5. _____   6. 4 _____

7. _____   8. _____   *and* _____

Riding over the bump must have kicked up some dust.

Scholastic Teaching Resources

Use two list words to make a rhyme.

1. We hit a _____ on our way to the _____.

2. Will you give my back a _____ while I sit in the warm _____?

3. Achoo! I really _____ begin to _____.

4. These cookies are great! When I _____, I will bring _____.

Use the clues to identify the list words. Move the jeeps along the road by shading the answers. The jeep that reaches the end of the road first is the winner!

5. more than one

6. the past tense of *is*

7. a verb that rhymes with *cub*

8. starts like *friend*

9. jump – j + d

10. dirt

11. Change the vowel in *most*.

12. starts like *candy*

13. a noun that rhymes with *cub*

14. a _____ in the road

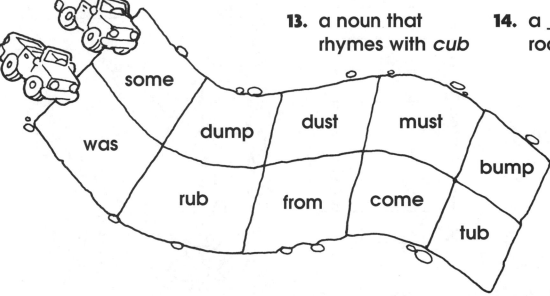

some
was
dump
dust
must
rub
from
come
bump
tub

Draw a picture to show each challenge word. Label the picture.

Scholastic Teaching Resources

Who Dropped the Ball?

Each of these words has a short vowel spelling with one final consonant. Before adding an ending like -ing or -ed, double the final consonant.

Read and copy each list word. Circle the letter that makes the short vowel sound. Underline the words with double consonants.

List Words

				words with no ending	words with an -ed ending
1.	tap	1.	_____		
2.	tapping	2.	_____	_____	_____
3.	beg	3.	_____	_____	_____
4.	begged	4.	_____	_____	
5.	skip	5.	_____	_____	words with an -ing ending
6.	skipping	6.	_____	_____	
7.	drop	7.	_____		_____
8.	dropped	8.	_____		_____
9.	run	9.	_____		_____
10.	running	10.	_____		_____

Challenge Words

11.	clapped	11.	_____
12.	tripped	12.	_____
13.	stopping	13.	_____

Unscramble the letters to spell list words.

1. nunigrn _____   2. dgebge _____

3. propedd _____   4. spik _____

5. snigippk _____ 6. patnpig _____

 She <u>dropped</u> the ball when she was <u>running</u> and <u>skipping</u>.

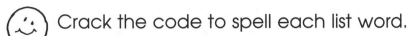 Write four sentences using at least two list words in each.

1. _____

2. _____

3. _____

4. _____

Crack the code to spell each list word.

a	b	d	e	g	i	k	n	o	p	r	s	t	u
☆	✧	✓	⊙	✺	✪	⏰	★	⇧	◯	✕	⧖	▢	☀

5. _ _ _ _ _ _ _
   ✓ ✕ ⇧ ◯ ◯ ⊙ ✓

6. _ _ _ _
   ⧖ ⏰ ✪ ◯

7. _ _ _ _ _ _ _ _
   ⧖ ⏰ ✪ ◯ ◯ ✪ ★ ✺

8. _ _ _
   ✕ ☀ ★

9. _ _ _ _ _ _ _
   ✕ ☀ ★ ★ ✪ ★ ✺

10. _ _ _ _
    ✓ ✕ ⇧ ◯

11. _ _ _
    ▢ ☆ ◯

12. _ _ _ _ _ _ _
    ▢ ☆ ◯ ◯ ✪ ★ ✺

13. _ _ _ _ _ _
    ✧ ⊙ ✺ ✺ ⊙ ✓

14. _ _ _
    ✧ ⊙ ✺

 Write the challenge word that belongs in each group.

clap, clapping,	stop, stopped,	trip, tripping,

 On another sheet of paper, make a word search puzzle using the list words. Ask a friend to find the hidden words.

Scholastic Teaching Resources

A Snake on the Trail

 The **long-**a **sound** *can be spelled with the letters* a_e, ai *, or* ay.

Read and copy each list word. Circle the letters that make the long-*a* sound. Watch for a word with an unexpected spelling. Then organize the list words by the letters making the long-*a* sound.

List Words

1. say
2. made
3. snake
4. pain
5. away
6. trade
7. train
8. brake
9. trail
10. they

	a_e	ai
1. _____	_____	_____
2. _____	_____	_____
3. _____	_____	_____
4. _____		_____
5. _____		**ay**
6. _____	**unexpected spelling**	_____
7. _____		_____
8. _____	_____	
9. _____		
10. _____		

Challenge Words

11. raise   11. _____
12. plate   12. _____
13. scrape   13. _____

Write three list words that rhyme with one another.

1. _____   _____   _____

Six other list words have a rhyming partner. Write them below.

2. _____   3. _____   4. _____

 Did <u>they</u> <u>say</u> the <u>snake</u> on the <u>trail</u> went <u>away</u>?

Scholastic Teaching Resources

📖 Use the list words to complete the letter.

Dear John,

My family went _____ for vacation. We took a _____ to Arizona.

My favorite part was riding horses. We followed a _____ into the desert.

Suddenly my horse had to _____. He saw a _____ on the trail. The

snake was hurt and in _____. I didn't know what to _____. "Stop!"

I called. The others _____ their horses stop. _____ saw the snake,

too. We used a stick to move the snake under a rock. I hope he'll be okay.

Your friend,
Joe

P.S. Do you want to _____ baseball cards?

😊 Follow the clues to complete the puzzle.

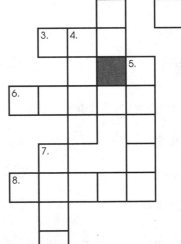

Across
2. rhymes with *sale*
3. to speak
6. a form of transportation
8. a synonym for *swap*
9. the past tense of *make*

Down
1. feel this when you are hurt
2. a list word with an unexpected spelling
4. rhymes with *day*
5. a reptile
7. a synonym for *stop*

 Write the challenge word that finishes each analogy.

1. Lower is to move down as _____ is to move up.

2. Cut is to finger as _____ is to knee.

3. Drink is to cup as eat is to _____.

 On another sheet of paper, scramble the letters in each list word. Ask a friend to unscramble the words.

A Sleepy Team

 The **long**-e **sound** *can be spelled with the letters* e_e, ea, *or* ee.

Read and copy each list word. Circle the letters that make the long-*e* sound. Then organize the list words by the letters making the long-*e* sound.

List Words

1. meet
2. each
3. here
4. read
5. seen
6. team
7. wheel
8. mean
9. eve
10. sleep

	e_e		**ee**
1. _____			_____
2. _____			_____
3. _____			_____
4. _____	*ea*		_____
5. _____	_____		
6. _____	_____		
7. _____	_____		
8. _____	_____		
9. _____			
10. _____			

Challenge Words

11. these
12. easy
13. please

11. _____
12. _____
13. _____

Change one letter in each word to spell a list word. The first one has been done for you.

1. sheep ___sleep___
2. been _____
3. melt _____
4. meal _____
5. tear _____
6. road _____
7. hare _____
8. ewe _____

Change the first and last letters to spell a list word.

9. sheet _____
10. back _____

Each week the team reads here.

Scholastic Teaching Resources

Circle ten misspelled words. Write them correctly on the lines below.

A Sleepy Team

Last weak our gymnastics teem met heer. Eech boy and girl had to practice harder than before. We worked as hard as a hamster running on a weel. We did not even have a chance to sleap. At first we thought our coach was meen, but now I have sean what extra work can do for our team. We are all tired, but we are ready for our first gymnastics meet on New Year's Eev. You can rede about it in the newspaper. I hope we do well!

1. _____   2. _____

3. _____   4. _____

5. _____   6. _____

7. _____   8. _____

9. _____   10. _____

 Use addition and subtraction to spell each list word.

11. swan − sw + me = _____   12. sell − ll + en = _____

13. help − lp + re = _____   14. she − sh + ve = _____

15. rest − st + ad = _____   16. creep − cr + sl = _____

17. wheat − at + el = _____   18. well − ll + ek = _____

19. itch − it + ea = _____   20. clam − cl + te = _____

 Write the challenge word that matches each definition.

21. simple _____

22. used with a request, to show good manners _____

23. used before a plural noun _____

 On another sheet of paper, make a word search puzzle using the list words.

Scholastic Teaching Resources

The Night Sky

 *The **long-**i **sound** can be spelled with the letters* i_e, igh, *or* y.

Read and copy each list word. Circle the letters that make the long-*i* sound. Watch for a word that has an unexpected spelling. Then organize the list words by the letters making the long-*i* sound.

List Words

		i_e	**y**
1. sky	**1.** _____	_____	_____
2. time	**2.** _____	_____	_____
3. right	**3.** _____	_____	_____
4. night	**4.** _____	_____	_____
5. cry	**5.** _____	**igh**	
6. wide	**6.** _____	_____	
7. try	**7.** _____	_____	
8. light	**8.** _____	_____	
9. slide	**9.** _____		
10. why	**10.** _____		

Challenge Words

11. while	**11.** _____
12. bright	**12.** _____
13. stripe	**13.** _____

 Circle the word that is spelled correctly.

1. slyde	slide	**2.** try	trie	**3.** nite	night
4. right	ryte	**5.** skye	sky	**6.** light	lite
7. wide	wyde	**8.** cry	crie	**9.** whi	why

 "That's **right**. The **light** in the **night sky** is the moon."

Scholastic Teaching Resources

Write the list word that matches each clue.

1. I am the antonym for *day*. I am _____.

2. Children sit on me at the park. I am a _____.

3. I begin with the same sound as *truck*. I am _____.

4. I am used to ask a question. I am _____.

5. I am a synonym for *weep*. I am _____.

6. I am an antonym for *narrow*. I am _____.

7. We rhyme with *bite*. We are _____ and _____.

8. I am always above you. I am the _____.

9. I tell past, present, and future. I am _____.

Circle each list word hidden in the puzzle. The words go across, down, or diagonally.

a	q	w	t	s	l	i	d	e	c	r
t	t	r	i	d	j	i	s	s	k	w
r	p	i	e	d	i	u	g	b	k	h
y	l	g	m	y	e	w	o	h	i	y
m	f	h	v	e	n	i	g	h	t	s
i	n	t	i	l	h	t	g	c	r	y

Write the challenge word that finishes each sentence.

10. My teacher said, "The American flag has 13 _____s."

11. "Did it rain _____ you were at the beach?" she asked.

12. Michael shouted, "I have a _____ idea!"

 On another sheet of paper, write a story using as many list words as possible.

Let It Snow!

 *The **long-**o **sound** can be spelled with the letters* o_e, oa, *or* ow.

Read and copy each list word. Circle the letters that make the long-*o* sound. Watch for a word that has an unexpected silent letter. Then organize the list words by the letters making the long-*o* sound.

 List Words

			o_e	ow
1.	toad	1. _____	_____	_____
2.	grow	2. _____	_____	_____
3.	nose	3. _____	_____	_____
4.	boat	4. _____		
5.	snow	5. _____	oa	
6.	broke	6. _____	_____	
7.	close	7. _____	_____	
8.	soap	8. _____	_____	
9.	coat	9. _____	_____	
10.	know	10. _____		

🏆 **Challenge Words**

11.	show	11. _____
12.	wrote	12. _____
13.	those	13. _____

👀 Can you find all ten list words hidden two times? Circle them.

brocoatknsoapow   noknowplbrokese   boclosewtoadoatn

snowabrokeknow   bogrowboatlosen   clonosegrowocoat

closeknosnowese   knonoseowsoape   toadyowboatnown

 Did <u>you</u> <u>know</u> she <u>broke</u> her <u>nose</u> in the <u>snow</u>?

Scholastic Teaching Resources

Use a list word to complete each analogy.

1. *Bathing suit* is to *summer* as _____ is to *winter*.

2. A *train* is to *tracks* as a _____ is to *water*.

3. A *knob* is to *door* as a _____ is to *face*.

4. *See* is to *saw* as *break* is to _____.

5. *Rain* is to *warm* as _____ is to *cold*.

6. A *tiger* is to *mammal* as a _____ is to *amphibian*.

7. *Drink* is to *drank* as _____ is to *knew*.

8. *Shampoo* is to *hair* as _____ is to *body*.

Use the clues to identify the list words. Move the sleds down the hill by circling the answers. The sled that reaches the bottom first is the winner!

9. to get bigger

10. used to smell

11. used to clean

12. knit – it + ow

13. antonym for *open*

14. a type of transportation

15. chow – ch + sn

16. used to keep warm

grow

soap

nose

close

know

boat

coat

snow

Write each challenge word three times.

_____   _____   _____

_____   _____   _____

_____   _____   _____

Deep in the Hole

 Some of the common spellings for **long vowel sounds** *are:*

| a_e | e_e | i_e | o_e |
| ai, ay | ea, ee | y, igh | oa, ow |

Read and copy each list word. Circle the letters that make the long vowel sound. Then organize the list words by their long vowel sounds.

 List Words   long-*a* sound   long-*i* sound

1. deep   1. _____   _____   _____
2. hole   2. _____   _____   _____
3. ride   3. _____   _____
4. meal   4. _____   long-*o* sound
5. snail   5. _____
6. blow   6. _____   long-*e* sound   _____
7. game   7. _____   _____   _____
8. lay   8. _____
9. goat   9. _____
10. might   10. _____

Challenge Words

11. globe   11. _____
12. became   12. _____
13. smile   13. _____

Unscramble the letters to spell list words.

1. bowl _____   2. alins _____   3. mega _____
4. alem _____   5. yal _____   6. deir _____
7. tago _____   8. leoh _____   9. githm _____
   10. eped _____

 The snail might lay deep in the hole.

Write four sentences using at least two list words.

1. _____

2. _____

3. _____

4. _____

 Crack the code to spell each list word.

1	2	3	4	5	6	7	8	9	10	11	12	13	14	15	16	17
g	a	w	r	s	n	i	l	y	d	p	o	t	b	m	h	e

5. 1–2–15–17

_____

6. 16–12–8–17

_____

7. 8–2–9

_____

8. 15–17–2–8

_____

9. 1–12–2–13

_____

10. 10–17–17–11

_____

11. 15–7–1–16–13

_____

12. 4–7–10–17

_____

13. 14–8–12–3

_____

14. 5–6–2–7–8

_____

 Write the challenge word that belongs in each group.

become, becoming,	map, atlas,	smirk, frown,

 On another sheet of paper, write a definition for each list word.

The Cute Mule

 *The **long-u sound** can be spelled with the letters* oo *or* u_e.

Read and copy each list word. Circle the letters that make the long-*u* sound. Watch for a word that has an unexpected spelling. Organize the list words by the letters making the long-*u* sound.

List Words

		oo	u_e
1. room	1. _____	_____	_____
2. food	2. _____	_____	_____
3. tube	3. _____	_____	_____
4. mule	4. _____	_____	_____
5. moon	5. _____		_____
6. rule	6. _____	unexpected spelling	
7. spoon	7. _____		
8. cute	8. _____	_____	
9. tune	9. _____		
10. who	10. _____		

Challenge Words

11. school	11. _____
12. goose	12. _____
13. scooter	13. _____

Change one letter in each word to spell a list word.

1. cube _____ *or* _____   2. zoom _____

3. tube _____   4. why _____   5. role _____

6. spook _____   7. noon _____   8. fool _____

9. male _____

Who saw the cute mule eating his food?

Scholastic Teaching Resources

Name _____

 Use a list word to complete each sentence.

1. A _____ is a mammal similar to a donkey.

2. There is a _____ baby mule at the zoo.

3. The baby mule gets anxious when he wants _____.

4. He has plenty of _____ to play in his pen.

5. One zoo _____ is that visitors cannot feed the mule.

6. The _____ revolves around Earth.

7. _____ is going to the football game?

8. My baby sister has learned to eat with a _____.

9. Have you heard this _____ before?

10. I found a _____ of toothpaste in my suitcase.

 Follow the clues to complete the puzzle.

Across

2. rhymes with *groom*

5. a breakfast utensil

8. the base word of *ruler*

10. a synonym for *song*

Down

1. a question word

3. seen in the night sky

4. bread, fruit, vegetables

6. a stubborn mammal

7. an antonym for *ugly*

9. rhymes with *cube*

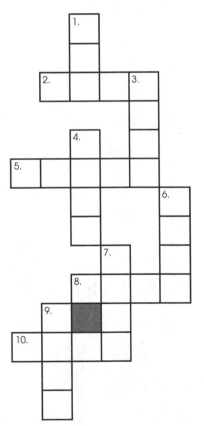

 Write the challenge word that finishes each analogy.

11. A unicycle has one wheel. A _____ has two wheels.

12. A baby cow is a calf. A baby _____ is a gosling.

13. We play on a playground. We learn in a _____.

 On another sheet of paper, write the list words in order from easiest to hardest to spell.

A True Blue Friend

When the **long-u sound** is found at the end of a word, it can be spelled with the letters ew *or* ue.

Read each list word. Circle the letters that make the long-*u* sound. Watch for a word that has an unexpected spelling. Then organize the list words by the letters making the long-*u* sound.

List Words

			ew	*ue*
1. few	**1.** _____		_____	_____
2. new	**2.** _____		_____	_____
3. true	**3.** _____		_____	_____
4. blue	**4.** _____		_____	
5. grew	**5.** _____		_____	
6. flew	**6.** _____		_____	
7. glue	**7.** _____			unexpected spelling
8. drew	**8.** _____			
9. threw	**9.** _____			_____
10. two	**10.** _____			

Challenge Words

11. due	**11.** _____
12. dew	**12.** _____
13. knew	**13.** _____

Change the first and last letters of each word to spell a list word.

1. grub _____ **2.** owl _____ **3.** let _____ *and* _____

4. sled _____ **5.** club _____ *and* _____

 The bluebird <u>flew</u> over a <u>few</u> <u>new</u> flowers.

Circle ten misspelled words. Write them correctly on the lines.

A True Blue Friend

"Today was a great day at school," Mark said as he thrue the door open. He sat down at the table and took a fue grapes from the bowl. "We drooe pictures to show the parts of a plant. Before I could glew my pictures in place, Drew walked by and brushed them onto the floor. I was so mad! I had to draw tow noow pictures! Then something pretty cool happened. Matthew came over and helped me. We flewe through the work together. I grue less angry then."

Mark's mom replied, "Matthew really is a troo blewe friend."

1. _____ 2. _____ 3. _____ 4. _____ 5. _____

6. _____ 7. _____ 8. _____ 9. _____ 10. _____

 Use addition and subtraction to spell each list word.

11. flag – ag + ew = _____   **12.** glad – ad + ue = _____

13. net – t + w = _____   **14.** toe – oe + wo = _____

15. drum – um + ew = _____   **16.** grip – ip + ew = _____

17. trap – ap + ue = _____   **18.** fur – ur + ew = _____

19. crew – c + th = _____   **20.** blob – ob + ue = _____

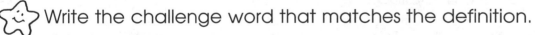 Write the challenge word that matches the definition.

21. drops of water sometimes found on grass early in the morning _____

22. something owed or expected to arrive _____

23. the past tense of *know* _____

 On another sheet of paper, write the list words in alphabetical order.

A Good Book

 The letters u, oo, and ou can all sound like oo in good.

Read and copy each list word. Circle the letters that make the short *oo* sound. Watch for three words that have unexpected spellings. Then organize the list words by the letters that make the short *oo* sound.

List Words

u

1. good   1. _____   _____
2. book   2. _____   _____
3. put   3. _____   _____
4. could   4. _____
5. look   5. _____   **oo**
6. pull   6. _____   _____
7. would   7. _____   _____
8. push   8. _____   _____
9. foot   9. _____   _____
10. should   10. _____

Challenge Words

11. stood   11. _____
12. shook   12. _____
13. cookbook 13. _____

Circle the word that is spelled correctly.

1. shood	should	2. louk	look	3. put	poot
4. foot	fout	5. cood	could	6. gude	good
7. pul	pull	8. book	booke	9. woud	would

"I should look for a good book," Eric said.

10. puch   push

Name _____

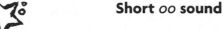

Write the list word that matches each clue.

1. I am the antonym for *push*. I am _____.

2. When I am plural, I become *feet*. I am _____.

3. I have a homonym that is spelled *wood*. I am _____.

4. Use your eyes to do this. I am _____.

5. I am a synonym for *shove*. I am _____.

6. I am a noun. I am made of paper. I am a _____.

7. I am a three-letter word. I am _____.

8. I am less than *great*. I am _____.

9. We rhyme with *good*. We are _____, _____, and _____.

 Circle each list word hidden in the puzzle. The words go across, down, or diagonally.

g	p	u	s	h	k	w	p	u	t	f
b	p	u	o	h	s	b	l	c	j	o
o	h	c	l	n	o	i	r	o	t	o
o	l	q	v	l	d	u	b	u	o	t
k	w	o	u	l	d	c	l	l	a	k
f	m	e	d	s	g	o	o	d	t	l

Write the challenge word that finishes each exclamation.

10. We _____ on the back of a dolphin!

11. The earthquake _____ the house!

12. This is a great _____!

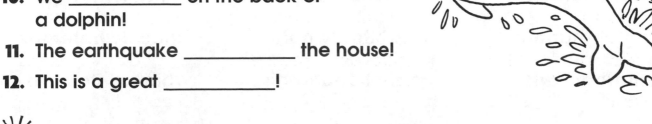

 Find each of the list words in a few of your favorite books.

Scholastic Teaching Resources

Which White Shell?

➡️ *In some words, two letters work together to make one sound.*

Read and copy each list word. Circle the letters that make a new sound.
Then organize the list words by the letters that make the new sound.

 List Words

1. wish
2. chase
3. shell
4. shut
5. than
6. chat
7. white
8. them
9. which
10. what

🏆 **Challenge Words**

11. there
12. where
13. these

1. _____
2. _____
3. _____
4. _____
5. _____
6. _____
7. _____
8. _____
9. _____
10. _____
11. _____
12. _____
13. _____

sh
_____
_____
_____
_____

ch
_____
_____
_____

th
_____
_____
_____

wh
_____
_____
_____

wh and ch
_____

👀 Can you find all ten list words hidden two times? Circle them.

awshellchwisht   thchasethemack   whshutshchatn

whichthannth   shwhiteafwhatin   chasetwhatente

shutthanewish   prshellenchathir   whichwhitethem

 Which white shell will you give **them**?

Use a list word to complete each analogy.

1. To trot is to run. To _____ is to talk.

2. Grass is green. Snow is _____.

3. *Him* means one person. _____ means many people.

4. A rock is found in the dirt. A _____ is found in the ocean.

5. *High* is the antonym for *low*. _____ is the antonym for *open*.

6. *See* is a homonym for *sea*. _____ is a homonym for *witch*.

7. *Chair* rhymes with *hair*. *Pan* rhymes with _____.

8. To run fast is to scurry. To run after is to _____.

9. Make a play in a game. Make a _____ on a star.

10. *Hat* rhymes with *that*. *Hut* rhymes with _____ and _____.

 Complete each puzzle with two list words.

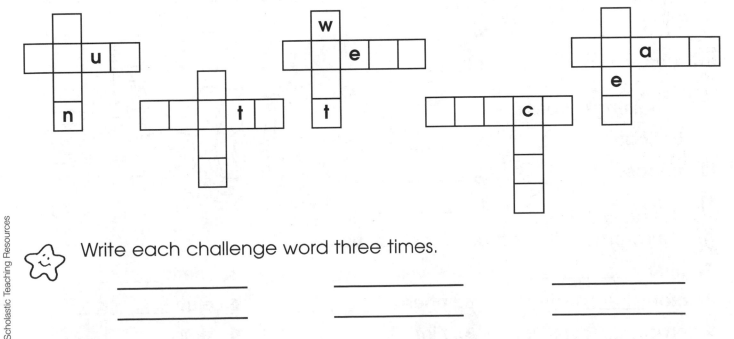

 Write each challenge word three times.

_____   _____   _____

_____   _____   _____

_____   _____   _____

 Find each list word in a dictionary. On another sheet of paper, write the list word and the page number where it was found.

Scholastic Teaching Resources

A Clue to the Treasure Chest

➡️ *In some words two letters work together to make one sound. The **long-u sound** can be spelled with the letters oo, u_e, ew, and ue. The **short** oo sound can be spelled with the letters u, oo, and ou.*

Read and copy each list word. Watch for a word that has an unexpected spelling. Then organize the list words by the listed sounds.

📝 **List Words**

1. bush
2. tool
3. thin
4. blew
5. chest
6. took
7. brush
8. shape
9. clue
10. whale

1. _____
2. _____
3. _____
4. _____
5. _____
6. _____
7. _____
8. _____
9. _____
10. _____

long-u sound as in *room*

_____
_____
_____
_____

short oo sound as in *good*

_____
_____
_____

ch, th, wh, or sh

_____
_____
_____
_____
_____

🏆 **Challenge Words**

11. balloon
12. choose
13. shoe

11. _____
12. _____
13. _____

👓 Unscramble the letters to spell list words.

1. alhew _____
2. sbuhr _____
3. shetc _____
4. olot _____
5. phesa _____
6. eluc _____
7. elwb _____
8. niht _____
9. shub _____
10. okot _____

 The <u>clue</u> says, "Use the <u>tool</u> to open the <u>chest</u>."

Scholastic Teaching Resources

Write four sentences using at least two list words in each.

1. _____

2. _____

3. _____

4. _____

Riddle time! Use the clues to write each list word in the boxes. When you have finished, the shaded boxes will spell the answer to the riddle.

What has ten letters and starts with gas?

1. A square is a _____.

2. rhymes with *blue*

3. a part of the body

4. past tense of *take*

5. a hammer

6. a plant

7. antonym for *thick*

8. an ocean animal

9. homonym for *blue*

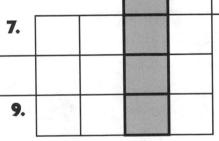

 Write the challenge word that belongs in each group.

sock, boot,	decide, pick,	circus, clown,

On another sheet of paper, make a word search puzzle using the list words. Ask a friend to find all ten words.

The Hurt Bird

 The sound a vowel makes often changes when it is followed by an r.

Read and copy each list word. Circle the "vowel plus *r*" spellings. Watch for words that have unexpected spellings. Then organize the list words by the number of letters they have.

List Words

1. smart
2. her
3. bird
4. more
5. curl
6. sharp
7. were
8. first
9. hurt
10. your

three letters   **five letters**

1. _____   _____   _____
2. _____   _____
3. _____   **four letters**
4. _____   _____
5. _____   _____
6. _____   _____
7. _____   _____
8. _____   _____
9. _____   _____
10. _____

Challenge Words

11. morning
12. third
13. before

11. _____
12. _____
13. _____

Write a list word that begins with the same sound as the picture.

1. _____   2. _____ *and* _____

3. _____   4. _____   5. _____

6. _____   7. _____   8. _____

 Was <u>your</u> <u>bird</u> <u>hurt</u> by the <u>sharp</u> stick?

Scholastic Teaching Resources

 Circle ten misspelled words. Write them correctly on the lines.

Kia was given a berd for her eighth birthday. She named her Sweetie. It was the forst pet Kia had ever had. Sometimes Kia's bird would sit on hir shoulder. "Yor bird is really smurt," everyone told Kia. One day Kia and Sweetie wer sitting on the front porch. A wild bird with a cirl on its head landed nearby. Sweetie flew from Kia's shoulder and onto a branch near the wild bird. The wild bird flew away. Kia waited for Sweetie to fly back, but her bird didn't. Sweetie seemed to be hert. Kia lifted Sweetie down and noticed how sharpe the branch was. Kia said, "You can't fly with the wild birds. They have mor experience than you do, Sweetie." The bird seemed to understand and climbed back onto Kia's shoulder.

1. _____ 2. _____ 3. _____ 4. _____

5. _____ 6. _____ 7. _____ 8. _____

9. _____ 10. _____

Follow the clues to play tic-tac-toe. As you find each answer, mark an *X* or *O*. Do you get three in a row?

11. I am the antonym for *dull*. Mark an *O*.

12. I begin like the word *birthday*. Mark an *X*.

13. I come before *second*. Mark an *O*.

14. I am the antonym for *less*. Mark an *X*.

15. I show that a girl owns something. Mark an *O*.

16. I am a synonym for *intelligent*. Mark an *X*.

17. I rhyme with *shirt*. Mark an *O*.

18. I rhyme with *her*. Mark an *X*.

19. I describe a pig's tail. Mark an *O*.

her	were	hurt
bird	curl	smart
first	more	sharp

Draw a picture to illustrate each challenge word. Label the picture.

Name _____ Diphthongs *ow* and *ou*

The Clown's House

 In some words, vowel combinations come together to make a completely new sound. The letters ou *and* ow *often make the same sound. For example:* **out** *and* **cow**

Read and copy each list word. Circle the *ou* or *ow* spelling. Then organize the list words by either *ou* or *ow*.

 List Words   **ou**   **ow**

 1. how   1. _____   _____   _____
 2. clown   2. _____   _____   _____
 3. house   3. _____   _____   _____
 4. down   4. _____   _____   _____
 5. now   5. _____   _____   _____
 6. shout   6. _____
 7. about   7. _____
 8. town   8. _____
 9. count   9. _____
10. our   10. _____

Challenge Words

11. found   11. _____
12. crown   12. _____
13. mouth   13. _____

Change the last two letters in each word to spell a list word.

 1. shore _____   2. abode _____   3. his _____

 4. couch _____   5. torn _____   6. hound _____

 7. net _____   8. cloud _____   9. oat _____

 The **clown's** house is **downtown** near **our** **house**.   10. door _____

Scholastic Teaching Resources

38   Scholastic Success With Spelling • Grade 2

📖 Complete the story using each of the list words.

The circus has come to _____! My favorite part is watching the

_____ shoot out of the cannon. We all _____ from 10 _____ to

zero and then yell, "Blast off!" Then we cover _____ ears because the

cannon is loud. You can hear the clown _____, "Wheee," as he flies

over our heads. He flies for _____ two minutes. Then he disappears.

"Where is he _____?" everyone asks. Suddenly, the clown jumps out of

a dog's _____. "Wow! _____ did he do that?" we all wonder.

☺ Use the clues to identify the list words. Move the clowns along the path
by shading the answers. The clown that reaches the circus tent first is
the winner.

1. the antonym for *up*
2. Where is ____ dog?
3. a circus performer
4. at this time
5. a synonym for *home*
6. smaller than a city
7. 1, 2, 3 . . .
8. a question word
9. not exact
10. a synonym for *yell*

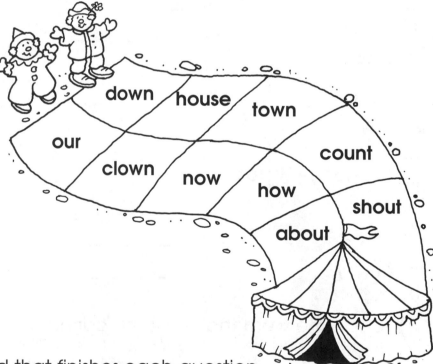

down house town
our count
clown now how
shout
about

⭐ Write the challenge word that finishes each question.

11. Has he _____ his notebook yet?

12. Can you talk with your _____ closed?

13. Did you notice all of the jewels in the ancient _____?

💡 Cut letters from an old newspaper and glue them to another sheet of paper to spell each of
the list words.

Enjoy the Toy!

The letters oi *and* oy *often make the same sound. For example:* oil *and* boy

Read and copy each list word. Circle the *oi* or *oy* spelling. Then organize the list words by either *oi* or *oy*.

 List Words   *oi*   *oy*

1. oil   1. _____   _____   _____

2. boy   2. _____   _____   _____

3. toy   3. _____   _____   _____

4. join   4. _____   _____   _____

5. soil   5. _____   _____

6. joy   6. _____   _____

7. boil   7. _____

8. enjoy   8. _____

9. coin   9. _____

10. point   10. _____

 Challenge Words

11. noise   11. _____

12. voice   12. _____

13. annoy   13. _____

 Circle the word that is spelled correctly.

1. joi   joy   2. soyl   soil   3. toy   toye

4. koin   coin   5. boy   boiy   6. joyn   join

7. enjoy   injoy   8. oil   oyl   9. boyl   boil

                                                 10. poynt   point

 The <u>boy</u> will <u>enjoy</u> the <u>toy</u> <u>coin</u>.

Scholastic Teaching Resources

📖 Use a list word to complete each analogy.

1. A fish lives in water. A flower lives in _____.

2. *Woman* is to *man* as *girl* is to _____.

3. *Cat* is to *at* as *boil* is to _____.

4. The nose is part of an airplane. The _____ is part of a pencil.

5. Water will freeze when it is cold. Water will _____ when it is hot.

6. *Rough* is the antonym of *smooth*. *Dislike* is the antonym of _____.

7. To separate is to break apart. To _____ is to come together.

8. Sadness is pain. Happiness is _____.

9. A tire is made of rubber. A _____ is made of metal.

10. A dog plays with a bone. A child plays with a _____.

😊 Use the Braille code to spell each list word.

b	c	e	i	j	l	n	o	p	s	t	y

11. ___ ___ ___ ___

12. ___ ___ ___ ___

13. ___ ___ ___ ___

14. ___ ___ ___

15. ___ ___ ___

16. ___ ___ ___ ___

17. ___ ___ ___ ___ ___

18. ___ ___ ___

19. ___ ___ ___ ___

20. ___ ___ ___ ___ ___

⭐ Write the challenge word that finishes each analogy.

21. *Scream* is a synonym for *yell*. *Bug* is a synonym for _____.

22. You walk with your feet. You sing with your _____.

23. You hear whispers in the library. You hear _____ on the playground.

💡 **Write a story using as many list words as possible.**

There Goes the Ball!

 The letters aw *make the sound in the word* **law***. The letters* all *make the sound in the word* **ball***. These are two different sounds.*

Read and copy each list word. Circle the *aw* or *all* spellings. Then organize the list words by either *aw* or *all*.

📝 **List Words**		*aw*	*all*
1. tall	**1.** _____	_____	_____
2. jaw	**2.** _____	_____	_____
3. ball	**3.** _____	_____	_____
4. hall	**4.** _____	_____	_____
5. paw	**5.** _____	_____	_____
6. saw	**6.** _____		
7. call	**7.** _____		
8. draw	**8.** _____		
9. yawn	**9.** _____		
10. fall	**10.** _____		

🏆 **Challenge Words**

11. dawn   **11.** _____

12. claw   **12.** _____

13. hawk   **13.** _____

 Write a list word that begins with the same letter as the picture.

1. _____   **2.** _____   **3.** _____

4.  _____   **5.** _____   **6.** _____

7. _____   **8.** _____   **9.** _____

 I <u>saw</u> the <u>ball</u> <u>fall</u> down the <u>hall</u>.

Scholastic Teaching Resources

Write the list word that matches each clue.

1. I am an animal's foot. I am a _____.

2. You do this when you are sleepy. I am a _____.

3. I am part of your face. I am a _____.

4. I am a season called autumn. I am _____.

5. I am an antonym for *short*. I am _____.

6. I am the past tense for *see*. I am _____.

7. I am shaped like a sphere. I am a _____.

8. I am the present tense of *drew*. I am _____.

9. I may be part of your school or house. I am a _____.

10. Your mother may do this at dinnertime. She may _____ you.

Circle each list word hidden in the puzzle. The words go across, down, or diagonally.

r	h	j	p	d	c	f	a	l	l	d
b	t	a	y	p	a	w	b	j	a	r
c	y	b	l	f	l	t	l	a	c	a
d	a	h	c	l	l	y	a	w	l	w
k	w	s	a	w	s	f	s	l	p	l
f	n	e	a	l	l	r	j	p	l	l

Change the last two letters in each word to spell a challenge word.

11. clip _____

12. hand _____

13. damp _____

 On another sheet of paper, write the list words in rhyming groups. Brainstorm more rhyming words for each list and write them.

The Girl's Small Horse

 Many letters may work together to make a new sound.
Remember these: ar er ir or ur ou ow aw all oi oy

Read and copy each list word. Circle the letters that work together. Then organize the list words by their vowel sounds.

📝 List Words

1. art	1. _____	**words with vowel + r**
2. straw	2. _____	_____
3. girl	3. _____	_____
4. south	4. _____	_____
5. small	5. _____	_____
6. horse	6. _____	_____
7. frown	7. _____	
8. sister	8. _____	
9. turn	9. _____	
10. foil	10. _____	

words with all or *aw*
_____
_____
_____

word with *oi*
_____

words with ou or *ow*
_____
_____

🏆 Challenge Words

11. purple   11. _____

12. round   12. _____

13. shirt   13. _____

👀 Unscramble the letters to spell list words.

1. rat _____   2. ilof _____   3. stohu _____

4. nutr _____   5. mlsla _____   6. ritses _____

7. norwf _____   8. resoh _____   9. wasrt _____

📣 The <u>small</u> <u>girl</u> may <u>frown</u> when she sees the <u>horse</u> <u>turn</u>.   10. ligr _____

Write four sentences using at least two list words in each.

1. _____

2. _____

3. _____

4. _____

 Riddle time! Use the clues to write each list word in the boxes. When you have finished, the shaded boxes will spell the answer to the riddle.

What do you call a crazy spaceman?

1. helps you take a drink
2. change directions
3. antonym for *big*
4. an animal
5. a class at school
6. antonym for *boy*
7. wrap food in this
8. rhymes with *clown*
9. a direction
10. a girl in your family

Write the challenge word that belongs in each group.

yellow, blue,	square, rectangular,	shoes, pants,

On another sheet of paper, write the definition for each of the list words.

Name _____

Master Spelling List

about	clap	foot	light	pick	slide	tool
after	close	fox	lock	point	slip	town
art	clown	from	look	pull	small	toy
ask	clue	frown	made	push	smart	trade
away	coat	game	map	put	snail	trail
ball	coin	girl	mask	read	snake	train
bed	come	glue	meal	ride	snow	true
beg	could	goat	mean	right	soap	try
begged	count	good	meet	room	sock	tub
bend	cry	grew	met	rub	soil	tube
best	curl	grow	might	rule	some	tune
bird	cute	hall	milk	run	south	turn
black	deep	has	miss	running	spoon	two
blew	dot	have	mix	sack	spot	was
blow	down	her	moon	said	stop	went
blue	draw	here	mop	saw	straw	were
boat	drew	hid	more	say	tall	whale
boil	drop	hole	mule	seen	tap	what
book	dropped	horse	must	send	tapping	wheel
box	dump	house	nest	shape	team	which
boy	dust	how	new	sharp	tent	white
brake	each	hurt	night	shell	than	who
broke	enjoy	jaw	nose	should	them	why
brush	eve	join	now	shout	they	wide
bump	fall	joy	odd	shut	thin	wish
bush	few	kick	off	sister	threw	with
call	first	kiss	oil	skip	time	would
chase	flew	know	our	skipping	tip	yawn
chat	foil	last	pain	sky	toad	yet
chest	food	lay	paw	sleep	took	your

Page 4
three letters: map, ask, has; four letters: last, sack, clap, mask, have; five letters: after, black; 2. mask; 3. clap; 4. black; 5. last; 6. map; 7. has; 8. sack; 9. have

Page 5
has; black; Last; have; ask; mask; map; clap; After; sack; 1. ask; 2. black; 3. last; 4. after; 5. has; 6. sack; 7. clap; 8. have; 9. mask; 10. stamp; 11. stand; 12. backpack

Page 6
t: tent, met, went, nest, yet, best; d: send, bed, bend, said; 1. tent, went; 2. met, yet; 3. send, bend; 4. bed, said; 5. nest, best

Page 7
1. tent; 2. bend; 3. best; 4. bed; 5. said; 6. nest; 7. send; 8. met; 9. went; 10. yet; 11. tent; 12. tent; 13. met; 14. bed; 15. send; 16. said; 17. bend; 18. yet; 19. nest; 20. went; 21. else; 22. bench; 23. next

Page 8
m: mix, milk, miss; p: tip, slip, pick; k: kick; kiss; h: hid, with; 1. pick; 2. milk; 3. kiss; 4. tip; 5. slip; 6. kick; 7. hid; 8. mix; 9. miss

Page 9
1. hid; 2. kick, pick; 3. milk; 4. with; 5. mix; 6. tip, slip; 7. kiss; 8. miss; 9. sister; 10. into; 11. trick

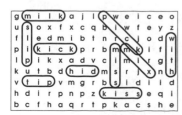

Page 10
sock, lock; mop, stop; box, fox; spot, dot; odd, off; 1. mop; 2. stop; 3. sock; 4. fox; 5. lock; 6. spot; 7. odd

Page 11
1. off; 2. sock; 3. mop; 4. lock; 5. box, fox; 6. stop; 7. odd; 8. dot; 9. spot; 10. sock, box; 11. spot, off; 12. lock, fox; 13. odd, dot; 14. stop, mop

Page 12
u: rub, bump, tub, dust, dump, must; o_e: come, some; a: was; o: from; 1. some; 2. must; 3. rub or bump; 4. bump; 5. was; 6. from; 7. come; 8. dump, dust

Page 13
1. bump, dump; 2. rub, tub; 3. must, dust; 4. come, some; 5. some; 6. was; 7. rub; 8. from; 9. dump; 10. dust; 11. must; 12. come; 13. tub; 14. bump

Page 14
no ending: tap, beg, skip, drop, run; -ed: begged, dropped; -ing: tapping, skipping, running; 1. running; 2. begged; 3. dropped; 4. skip; 5. skipping; 6. tapping

Page 15
5. dropped; 6. skip; 7. skipping; 8. run; 9. running, 10. drop; 11. tap; 12. tapping; 13. begged; 14. beg; clapped, stopping, tripped

Page 16
a_e: made, snake, trade, brake; ai: pain, train, trail; ay: say, away; unexpected spelling: they; 1. say, away, they; 2. made, trade; 3. snake, brake; 4. pain, train

Page 17
away, train, trail, brake, snake, pain, say, made, They, trade; 1. raise; 2. scrape; 3. plate

Page 18
e_e: here, eve; ea: each, read, team, mean; ee: meet, seen, wheel, sleep; 1. sleep; 2. seen; 3. meet; 4. mean; 5. team; 6. read; 7. here; 8. eve; 9. wheel; 10. each

Page 19
1. week; 2. team; 3. here; 4. Each; 5. wheel; 6. sleep; 7. mean; 8. seen; 9. Eve; 10. read; 11. mean; 12. seen; 13. here; 14. eve; 15. read; 16. sleep; 17. wheel; 18. week; 19. each; 20. team; 21. easy; 22. please; 23. these

Page 20
i_e: time, wide, slide; igh: right, night, light; y: sky, cry, try, why; 1. slide; 2. try; 3. night; 4. right; 5. sky; 6. light; 7. wide; 8. cry; 9. why

Page 21
1. night; 2. slide; 3. try; 4. why; 5. cry; 6. wide; 7. right, light; 8. sky; 9. time; 10. stripe; 11. while; 12. bright

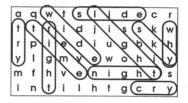

Page 22
o_e: nose, broke, close; oa: toad, boat, soap, coat; ow: grow, snow, know; coat, soap, know, broke; close, toad; snow, broke, know; grow, boat; nose, grow, coat; close, snow; nose, soap; toad, boat

Page 23
1. coat; 2. boat; 3. nose; 4. broke; 5. snow; 6. toad; 7. know; 8. soap; 9. grow; 10. nose; 11. soap; 12. know; 13. close; 14. boat; 15. snow; 16. coat

Page 24
long a: snail, game, lay; long e: deep, meal; long i: ride, might; long o: hole, blow, goat; 1. blow; 2. snail; 3. game; 4. meal; 5. lay; 6. ride; 7. goat; 8. hole; 9. might; 10. deep

Page 25
5. game; 6. hole; 7. lay; 8. meal; 9. goat; 10. deep; 11. might; 12. ride; 13. blow; 14. snail; became, globe, smile

Page 26
oo: room, food, moon, spoon; u_e: tube, mule, rule, cute, tune; unexpected spelling: who; 1. cute, tube; 2. room; 3. tune; 4. who; 5. rule; 6. spoon; 7. moon; 8. food; 9. mule

Scholastic Teaching Resources

Page 27

1. mule; 2. cute; 3. food;
4. room; 5. rule; 6. moon;
7. Who; 8. spoon; 9. tune;
10. tube; 11. scooter;
12. goose; 13. school

Page 28

ew: few, new, grew, flew,
drew, threw; eu: true, blue,
glue; unexpected spelling:
two; 1. true; 2. two; 3. new
and few; 4. flew; 5. blue
and glue

Page 29

1. threw; 2. few; 3. drew;
4. glue; 5. two; 6. new;
7. flew; 8. grew; 9. true;
10. blue; 11. flew; 12. glue;
13. new; 14. two; 15. drew;
16. grew; 17. true; 18. few;
19. threw; 20. blue;
21. dew; 22. due; 23. knew

Page 30

u: put, pull, push; oo: good,
book, look, foot; ou: could,
would, should;
1. should; 2. look; 3. put;
4. foot; 5. could; 6. good;
7. pull; 8. book; 9. would;
10. push

Page 31

1. pull; 2. foot; 3. would;
4. look; 5. push; 6. book;
7. put; 8. good; 9. could,
should, would; 10. stood;
11. shook; 12. cookbook

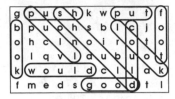

Page 32

sh: wish, shell, shut; ch:
chase, chat; th: than, them;
wh: white, what; wh and
ch: which; shell, wish;
chase, them; shut, chat;
which, than; white, what;
chase, what; shut, than,
wish; shell, chat; which,
white, them

Page 33

1. chat; 2. white; 3. Them;
4. shell; 5. Shut; 6. Which;
7. than; 8. chase; 9. wish;
10. shut, what

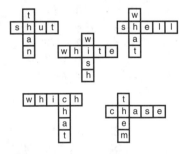

Page 34

room: tool, blew, clue;
good: bush, took; ch, th,
wh, or sh: bush, thin,
chest, brush, shape,
whale; 1. whale; 2. brush;
3. chest; 4. tool; 5. shape;
6. clue; 7. blew; 8. thin;
9. bush; 10. took

Page 35

1. shape; 2. clue; 3. chest;
4. took; 5. tool; 6. bush;
7. thin; 8. whale; 9. blew;
automobile; shoe, choose,
balloon

Page 36

three: her; four: bird, more,
curl, were, hurt, your; five:
smart, sharp, first;
1. smart; 2. her, hurt;
3. first; 4. were; 5. bird;
6. curl; 7. sharp; 8. more

Page 37

1. bird; 2. first; 3. her;
4. Your; 5. smart; 6. were;
7. curl; 8. hurt; 9. sharp;
10. more; 11. sharp;
12. bird; 13. first; 14. more;
15. her; 16. smart;
17. hurt; 18. were; 19. curl

Page 38

ou: house, shout, about,
count, our; ow: how, clown,
down, now, town;
1. shout; 2. about; 3. how;
4. count; 5. town; 6. house;
7. now; 8. clown;
9. our; 10. down

Page 39

town, clown, count, down,
our, shout, about, now,
house, How; 1. down;
2. our; 3. clown; 4. now;
5. house; 6. town;
7. count; 8. how; 9. about;
10. shout; 11. found;
12. mouth; 13. crown

Page 40

oi: oil, join, soil, boil, coin,
point; oy: boy, toy, joy,
enjoy; 1. joy; 2. soil; 3. toy;
4. coin; 5. boy; 6. join;
7. enjoy; 8. oil; 9. boil;
10. point

Page 41

1. soil; 2. boy; 3. oil;
4. point; 5. boil; 6. enjoy;
7. join; 8. joy; 9. coin;
10. toy; 11. oil; 12. coin;
13. boil; 14. toy; 15. boy;
16. soil; 17. enjoy; 18. joy;
19. join; 20. point;
21. annoy; 22. voice;
23. noise

Page 42

aw: jaw, paw, saw, draw,
yawn; tall: all, ball, hall,
call, fall; 1. saw; 2. jaw;
3. draw; 4. fall; 5. call;
6. ball; 7. hall; 8. paw;
9. yawn

Page 43

1. paw; 2. yawn; 3. jaw;
4. fall; 5. tall; 6. saw;
7. ball; 8. draw; 9. hall;
10. call; 11. claw;
12. hawk; 13. dawn

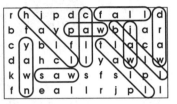

Page 44

vowel + r: art, girl, horse,
sister, turn; ou or ow:
south, frown; all or aw:
straw, small; oi: foil; 1. art;
2. foil; 3. south; 4. turn;
5. small; 6. sister; 7. frown;
8. horse; 9. straw; 10. girl

Page 45

1. straw; 2. turn; 3. small;
4. horse; 5. art; 6. girl;
7. foil; 8. frown; 9. south;
10. sister; an astronut;
purple, round, shirt